Jonathan Maitland

The Last Temptation of Boris Johnson

Salamander Street

PLAYS

First published in 2020 by Salamander Street Ltd.
(info@salamanderstreet.com.)

The Last Temptation of Boris Johnson © Jonathan Maitland, 2020

ISBN: 9781913630584

Printed and bound in Great Britain

10 9 8 7 6 5 4 3 2 1

Dramatis Personae
(Cast of 5.)

CAMERA OPERATOR

BORIS JOHNSON

HUW EDWARDS

MARINA WHEELER

EVGENY LEBEDEV

MICHAEL GOVE

SARAH VINE

MARGARET THATCHER

WINSTON CHURCHILL

TONY BLAIR

CAITLIN

THE CHAIRWOMAN OF THE
TORY PARTY (LEILA.)

JACK THE AGENT

Tracks

BORIS JOHNSON

CAMERA OPERATOR – MARINA WHEELER – CAITLIN

HUW EDWARDS – EVGENY LEBEDEV – TONY BLAIR

MICHAEL GOVE – WINSTON CHURCHILL – JACK THE AGENT

SARAH VINE – MARGARET THATCHER – LEILA

Act One

A tv space. A **CAMERA OPERATOR** *texts idly.* **BORIS** *appears, silhouetted in the doorway. Music: 'Should I Stay or Should I Go'*

HUW EDWARDS: The headlines tonight: a new poll shows the gap between the two sides in the forthcoming European Referendum, narrowing. Remain is still ahead, but by a margin of just over four per cent. We'll be talking to Boris Johnson, who still hasn't declared which side he'll campaign for, later in the programme.

HUW exits. **CAMERA OPERATOR** *touches headphones – the gallery's asking her where* **BORIS** *is. She talks to them via her lip mike.*

CAMERA OPERATOR: His press person said he'd be here five minutes ago … I've no idea! … I think so … yes of course I will. *(Looks up.)* Hold on. I think that's him now. Yup. It's him … okay!

BORIS *enters, head down, texting. He's charmless: not the confected bumbler once the* **CAMERA** *rolls.*

BORIS: Where do you want me?

CAMERA OPERATOR: Here?

In a hurry, she shows him his mark and brandishes a lapel mike.

CAMERA OPERATOR: In or out? Boris.

BORIS: What?

CAMERA OPERATOR: In, or out?

He clocks she's attractive. His demeanour changes: more friendly.

BORIS: That, is indeed, the question.

Beat. The **CAMERA OPERATOR** *chuckles slightly.*

CAMERA OPERATOR: So where do you want it?

BORIS: Let's go for 'out' shall we? But don't jump to conclusions. Who's doing the interview?

CAMERA OPERATOR: *(Attatching the mike.)* Huw Edwards.

BORIS: Oh God. When are we on?

CAMERA OPERATOR: Any minute now.

BORIS: Have you got a mirror?

> *She shows him one. He loosens his collar, musses his hair and untucks his shirt. She touches her earpiece.*

CAMERA OPERATOR: Coming to us in five.

> *The* **CAMERA OPERATOR** *exits.* **HUW EDWARDS** *appears.*

HUW: And now with the time just coming up to
    five minutes to seven –

BORIS: *(Sotto.)* Huw Bloody Edwards.

HUW: – you're watching BBC News. A proposed tourist attraction for London, the Garden Bridge, has been called "a complete and utter farce" following the revelation that it's cost more than forty million pounds of public money. Critics say the project is, quote, 'a colossal waste of money' One of its biggest supporters, the Mayor of London Boris Johnson, joins me now.

BORIS: Hello, Huw.

HUW: Is it a farce?

> **BORIS** *is transformed.*

BORIS: Well yes now look Huw absolutely not the bridge is a quite superb project which will greatly enhance the quality of life for millions of Londoners and tourists and I can tell you and your magnificent viewers that it's very much all systems go for this monumental project. Monumental! That's what it is Huw! Monumental.

HUW: Even though lots of people, very influential people, don't actually want it? Apart from Joanna Lumley.

BORIS: Yes well Joanna Lumley is a very fine woman but look 85% of Londoners want this thing, 85%, that's an incredible number, and for some reason, it does have some demented enemies but they just need to get behind it because this is gonna be absolutely great.

HUW: Now I have to ask about the referendum —

BORIS: — rather you didn't

HUW: — because campaigning starts soon as you know so have you made up your mind and if so can you put us out of our misery?

BORIS: Yes well when I do decide sadly you will not be the first person I shall inform Huw despite your charm, influence and may I say, George Clooney-esque good looks.

HUW: Because the polls are quite even at the moment and commentators say you're the one person who could swing it either way.

BORIS: Well I don't know about that but look this is far too important for one man, or woman, or what have you, to have that kind of influence that's just, twaddle, but look it's gonna be a good clean contest, no nastiness, harmony, indeed glutinous harmony, that's what it is, glutinous harmony, will break out everywhere. Like the New Seekers. I'd Like To Teach The World To Sing. In perfect harmony. D'you know that one?

HUW: Yes. So you haven't made up your mind.

BORIS: When I do you will you will be the first to know. Or the second. Whatever, whatevs!

HUW: Boris Johnson there.

BORIS: *(Sotto.)* Arsehole.

> **BORIS** *reverts to pre-interview mode, enters kitchen.*

HUW: Coming up in the next hour we take the temperature in Malvern *(Insert relevant town/city here.)* do people there, want in, or out of Europe. But first, Darren. With the weather.

> **HUW** *exits.* **BORIS** *enters his kitchen-diner and gazes at his Churchill book.*

MARINA: *(Off stage.)* Hello! Hello?

BORIS: *(Calling)* Marina? Darling? In the kitchen!

MARINA *enters, slightly flustered, puts down her legal briefs.*

MARINA: It's a kitchen supper tonight is that all right?

BORIS: Of course. What are we having?

MARINA: Lamb Stew. Remind me who's coming?

BORIS: The Goves, us, Evgeny Lebedev and – oh yeah guess who he's bringing.

MARINA: Don't tell me. Someone famous.

BORIS: Come on guess.

MARINA: I dunno. Dame, someone or other.

BORIS: Elizabeth. Hurley.

MARINA: What! Why?

BORIS: *(Shrugs.)* I dunno. He owns a newspaper for God's sake. He can invite anyone he likes.

MARINA: When are they due?

BORIS: Imminently.

MARINA: Right. What happened to your hand?

BORIS: Our oldest son, beat me at table tennis. First time ever. I, punched the wall.

> **MARINA** *tuts – she's used to this – and tends his hand.*

> *He's distracted/ agitated.*

MARINA: Are you all right?

> **BORIS** *doesn't respond.*

MARINA: Hello!!?

BORIS: Hm? What?

MARINA: Are you all right? You're not even in the room.

BORIS: I'm fine. I'm just, you know. Decisions. My head's full of bloody voices saying, different things.

MARINA: How are you going to play it tonight?

BORIS: You know what Gove's like. The wiles of Rasputin. The charm of Sacha Distel. The face of Joe 90.

MARINA: Just listen okay? Don't transmit, receive. Even if you are persuaded by him. Don't say yes to anything, 'til you've slept on it. There we go.

BORIS: All that matters is the end result.

MARINA: Exactly. That's all you need to think about. Where it's heading.

BORIS *picks up his Churchill book.* **MARINA** *carries on preparing.*

BORIS: My Winston book is number three on Amazon. Political Biographies. That twelve weeks in a row in the top ten.

The voice of **WINSTON.**

CHURCHILL: Alexander, Boris, de Pfeffel, Johnson. You are walking, with destiny.

BORIS: I know I am Winston.

MARINA: What?

BORIS: Nothing. Just – . Nothing.

Doorbell.

BORIS: Ah. Let us play.

BORIS *exits.*

EVGENY: *(Off stage.)* Boris!!

BORIS: The mighty Lebedev, of that ilk! Welcome to Islington Evgeny, my main man, my mainest of men!

BORIS *enters with* **EVGENY**, *who's showing him a bottle of wine.*

BORIS: Good God! No wonder you own half the world's media.

EVGENY: Marina! Always a pleasure.

EVGENY *air kisses* **MARINA** *and gives her the bottle.*

EVGENY: We were drinking this only yesterday. At my good friend Elton's. With Dame Helen Mirren. And Eddie Redmayne. Also, good friends.

MARINA: Gosh. Thank you!

BORIS: Where's Elizabeth?

EVGENY: Ah. Miss Hurley, regrets.

MARINA: That's a shame. Back in a moment.

   MARINA *exits.*

EVGENY: She sent this. Just now.

   EVGENY *shows text to* **BORIS**.

BORIS: Bloody hell. Three kisses from Liz Hurley!

EVGENY: She is also a good friend.

BORIS: You haven't – ? Have you?

   EVGENY *shakes his head.*

BORIS: There's not a man alive who wouldn't swap the deep deep peace of the marital double bed for the hurly burly of the chaise longue. With Hurley.

EVGENY: I will make it up to you. I will invite her to my next party in Italy. Good times will be had by all.

BORIS: Don't invite any journalists.

EVGENY: *(Taps nose.)* Your secrets are safe with me! How are your "technology lessons" going by the way?

BORIS: Yuh. Most enjoyable. I'm learning a lot. None of it to do with technology.

They laugh blokeishly /conspiratorially.

EVGENY: So. You have a very important decision to make. Come on. Give me a clue.

BORIS: I'm veering around like a bloody shopping trolley.

EVGENY: But in which, direction is this trolley, from, Waitrose? Hm? Going? The aisle specialising in European produce? Or the one which is more, British?

BORIS: I'm rather headed for the European aisle to be honest. What d'you think?

EVGENY: For me? Leave. No question. Why be a slave to Europe, when you can lead the world? Russia. America. China. AND? Great Britain. These are the world superpowers. You, and only you Boris, can put the 'Great', back into Britain. Because you are a great man.

BORIS: *(Deadly serious.)* Good point.

Doorbell.

BORIS: Ah. The Goves.

MARINA: *(Calling out, off stage.)* I'll get it!

MARINA *and* **MICHAEL** *enter.*

MICHAEL: Evgeny how lovely to see you.

EVGENY: Michael!

SARAH *enters.*

EVGENY: Sarah!

SARAH: Evgeny.

Light laughter. Drinks served.

MARINA: Apologies in advance if the food's a bit –. We're trying out a new au pair. It's the first time she's cooked for us.

SARAH: What happened to the old one?

BORIS: We got rid of her. Or rather Marina did.

MARINA: He finds it hard to sack people. To their face.

BORIS: I'd be useless on The Apprentice. Sir Alan: your job is safe for now. Look it's going to be a bit Culinarius Interruptus tonight. Letwin's ringing in. Wants me to, to line up with the Government.

MICHAEL: Hmm.

MARINA: Not a fan?

MICHAEL: I've watched his relentless rise, to the middle, with great interest.

Light laughter.

BORIS: The Gove blade made nary a sound as it entered the Letwin spine.

SARAH: *(Counting chairs.)* Who else is coming?

BORIS: Liz Hurley was. But isn't.

SARAH: Don't tell me. She couldn't find a suitable bikini.

EVGENY: She has lost a front row seat at history.

MARINA: Talking of which. Did you see that piece about Theresa May? Which way she's going.

MICHAEL: Theresa May. But then again, May not.

BORIS: But she probably will.

SARAH: That's cleared that up.

MICHAEL: Whereas Boris of course – ? *(Waits for reaction: doesn't get one.)* Have I told you my GDP story? Okay. So there was a public meeting somewhere about leaving the EU and one of the experts says to a woman in the audience, who wants to leave "did you know Madam, if we leave the EU, GDP will plummet by twelve per cent." And you know what she said? And pardon the language but this is exactly what she said, she said: "It's not my fucking GDP."

SARAH: So it's NOT the economy stupid.

BORIS: Hmm.

MICHAEL: She also said, she was, originally from India by the way which is relevant, she also said, how upset she was, about all the Poles who come over and get free health care and education and so on and then send their money back to Warsaw or wherever it is instead of –

SARAH: *(Interrupting)* Krakow! That's where ours comes from. Krakow.

MICHAEL: Quite. Anyway, the key thing, as this woman saw it, is why should Poles and Rumanians and so on get all the goodies when they've only just got here and may go back soon, when we've spent our entire lives here and laid down roots here. I call it "a hierarchy of belonging".

BORIS: You gonna use that line?

MICHAEL: Maybe.

SARAH: You should talk about Greece. All that fiscal waterboarding stuff. The EU's torturing them.

MICHAEL: Well quite.

SARAH: I said as much in my column last week.

MICHAEL: And very good it was too.

EVGENY: Even so Michael you have a problem with UKIP. They are toxic. They put people off.

MICHAEL: The Farraj problem.

EVGENY: Farridge. Nigel Farridge.

MICHAEL: No. Fa-raj. Definitely Fa-raj. How do you guys say it?

MARINA: We try not to.

EVGENY: Although, I think, Nigel Fa-. Nigel Fa-. Nigel, could go down in history as the most significant politician of the 21st century so far. Apart from you both of course. Michael and Boris.

BORIS and **MICHAEL** *nod in agreement.*

EVGENY: But, again: how do you deal, with the toxic problem? Nigel, is toxic.

MARINA: Quite. I mean it doesn't look good joining forces with someone who says he wouldn't live next door to Rumanians.

SARAH: Has he got a point?

BORIS: Not in Islington he hasn't. But, you know. Fuck Islington. I'll tell you how you deal with Farage. You treat him like a dangerous dog who's been let off the leash in the park. When it bites someone, someone you don't like, you just say, "Terribly sorry. He's not my dog. He's someone else's. Nothing to do with me." Then you go home and celebrate.

MARINA: Not that you're being cynical.

MICHAEL: In politics you sometimes have to hold your nose.

EVGENY: In other words, you can share a bed with someone. But you do not always have to have sex with them.

SARAH: It's called marriage. *(To **MICHAEL**.)* Just going to – . *('Freshen up'.)*

SARAH exits.

MARINA: Are you feeling strong Michael? You're going to get a lot of abuse over the next few weeks.

MICHAEL: I'm used to it. The other day someone said I looked like an old ventriloquist dummy that had just been discovered in the attic.

Mimes it – mild laughter.

BORIS: You should see what they say about me.

MICHAEL: Beware the 2am trawl through the internet. Did you see that one about you this morning Boris?

BORIS: No.

MICHAEL: *(Tapping mobile.)* Where is it. Ah yes. Actually. Moving on.

BORIS: No come on.

MICHAEL shows mobile to MARINA.

MICHAEL: Shall we let m'learned friend decide?

MARINA weighs up the tweet.

MARINA: "Yet another picture of Boris in his ridiculous running gear. If he really likes jogging so much why's he so fat?"

BORIS: Hrrgh.

MARINA: He has slimmed down recently. To be fair.

MICHAEL: I tell you what I will find difficult. Being centre stage these next few weeks. I don't mind being a supporting player. But I'd much rather someone else took the spotlight. And got the credit. Down the ages.

Pause.

BORIS: The Ladybird guide to Machiavelli. Chapter One.

Uneasy murmuring/chuckling.

MARINA: Right. Let's sit shall we.

The guests sit down.

BORIS: So! The last supper.

MICHAEL: The last supper before what?

EVGENY: Before all hell breaks loose.

MARINA: Ah. The potatoes. Boris. They're in the oven.

BORIS *opens oven.* **MARGARET THATCHER**'s *head appears in it.*

MARGARET: Hello Boris. It's Margaret. Lady Thatcher.

BORIS: *(Terrified.)* UUUURRRGGGH!

He slams it shut, looks at guests: they are frozen. He reopens

The over door. **MARGARET** *smiles. He slams it shut again.*

MARGARET: OPEN UP, NOW!

BORIS *slowly opens the oven door.*

BORIS: What do you want?

MARGARET: I want you to see sense. I want you leave Europe.

BORIS: Really?

MARGARET: We have lost control. Of our borders, our laws, and our destiny. It's gone too far.

BORIS: You started it.

MARGARET: I beg your pardon?

BORIS: You signed the Single European Act. 1986. It did what it said on the tin. Single, European, Act.

MARGARET: That was a trade agreement. Not the disgraceful betrayal of sovereignty that took place under my successor John Major. Or, as Dennis and I prefer to call him, Lord Haw-Haw. Take back control Boris. Take back control.

BORIS closes the door, opens it again – **MARGARET** *is gone, the potatoes are there. He brings them over to the table, dazed. The guests un-freeze.*

MARINA: Are you all right?

BORIS *in a daze.*

MICHAEL: A penny for them? Boris? Boris!

BORIS *snaps out of it.*

BORIS: We have lost control. Of our borders, our laws, and our destiny. It's gone too far.

MICHAEL: You're beginning to see the light.

EVGENY: The trolley is moving towards, the aisle with, the British cheese. And fish. And cold meats. Boris?

BORIS's *mobile rings.*

MARINA: It's Letwin. Boris!

BORIS: Hm?

MARINA: Oliver Letwin's on the phone.

Beat. **BORIS** *still in a daze.*

EVGENY: Maybe someone put Polonium Two Ten in his wine! A little, Russian humour.

MARINA: Boris. Answer your phone.

BORIS: Right. Yes. *(Answers it.)* Oliver? I'll call you back. *(Ends call.)*

Come on Gover. If we're not back in a week send a search party.

BORIS *and* **MICHAEL** *exit,* **SARAH** *enters.*

EVGENY: Will you pardon me also? My good friend Prince Andrew has a problem. *(Looks at mobile – his eyes widen.)* A very big problem.

EVGENY *exits.* **SARAH** *mimes picking objects off the floor.*

MARINA: What are you doing?

SARAH: Picking up all the names Evgeny's dropped. What's Letwin gonna say?

MARINA: He's got this, idea, about how we can take back sovereignty, but remain in the EU. Pie in the sky.

SARAH: Have you heard the joke about sovereignty? Think it's one of Boris's actually. Oh yes. Why is sovereignty like virginity? Coz once you've lost it you can never get it back. Ha! And Boris should know!

Silence.

SARAH: Shit. I'm really sorry.

You want to leave don't you?

(Slight panic.) Leave Europe I mean.

MARINA: Oh yes. EU rules, are like, a comfort blanket for terrorists. I see it at work every day. It's absurd. So has Michael actually told Number Ten, he's definitely joining leave?

SARAH: He thinks he has. But you know what Michael's like. He went to see David. Cameron. And said, something like, *(***MICHAEL*** type accent.)* "if it was anyone but you Dave, as Prime Minister, I would definitely campaign to leave the EU. But I have to say, I will find it very difficult to vote against you." And he comes home and says: "I've definitely told him, I'm definitely leaving." And I said, "Are you sure?" A few minutes later we get a call. Saying Dave's "delighted" that Michael's now, definitely ON side.

MARINA: Oh dear. Aren't you, God Mother to one of Samantha and David's kids?

SARAH: *(Nods.)* Florence. So it could be tricky. But it should be okay. Though why Michael feels such loyalty to Dave I don't know. Given it was Dave who sacked him from Education. That was a shabby day's work he might live to regret.

MARINA: Why is Michael so certain? Boris changes by the hour.

SARAH: His father? He went to see him last week in Scotland. He ran a fishing business his dad. It went bust coz of EU quotas. Michael went to see him to, you know, get his blessing. Which he got of course. I think when you're adopted you feel you owe your parents even more. It's Michael's revenge on the EU for ruining his dad's business. That's my theory.

MARINA: Does Michael want to be Prime Minister?

Beat.

SARAH: Noooo! Although you know what they say. "Every soldier has a Field Marshall's baton in his knap sack."

MARINA: What about every soldier's wife?

SARAH: Well. Hypothetically, obviously. I'd manage.

MARINA: How would you handle all the, hatred, coming at you, constantly?

SARAH: I write for the Daily Mail.

MARINA: Yes but they reserve a, special, place in hell for *(Mimes quote marks.)* "difficult" women married to Prime Ministers don't they. Look at Cherie.

SARAH: Oh yes! QC, like you! Mind you she brought it on herself.

MARINA: Double standard. I didn't see Dennis Thatcher getting crucified. They treated him like a hero.

SARAH: Yes but he didn't stick his head over the parapet all the time. Cherie was asking for it. All those houses. Would you, you know, get involved? If Boris was top dog.

MARINA: *(Nods.)* A lot needs changing. You wouldn't believe some of the things that go on. In and out of court.

SARAH: You could be Attorney General. Are there rules against that? Giving family members top jobs?

MARINA: Not if it's done on merit.

SARAH: My God. Imagine a cabinet full of Johnsons.

MARINA: You'd have to make the case. Which might be difficult with some of them. But they've all done pretty well out of him already haven't they? His family. Out of his name. His fame.

SARAH: You are so lo − .

Beat. **SARAH** *bites into her crispbread.*

MARINA: What? I'm so what?

SARAH: Nothing. How're they getting on d'you think?

MARINA: What were you going to say?

SARAH: Really?

MARINA: Really.

SARAH: I was going to say. *(Deep breath.)* Okay. You are so loyal.

MARINA: Why wouldn't I be?

SARAH: Don't make me say it.

MARINA: I won't be offended.

SARAH: Okay. How can you be so, loyal, to him. When he did what he did? So publically? I mean you handled it brilliantly of course.

MARINA: I made a choice. To be with him. And another. To stay and live with the consequences. But you don't have to stick with choices. In life or politics.

SARAH: Are you like this in court?

MARINA: *(Chuckles.)* And I did throw him out.

SARAH: I know.

MARINA: But then I thought about it. And forgave him. But if he ever did it again – .

Beat.

SARAH: If he was French they'd have made him President by now.

BORIS *enters.*

MARINA: How'd it go?

BORIS: Boringly.

MICHAEL: *(Off stage.)* Not at all Oliver!

BORIS: Talking of which –

MICHAEL *enters, talking into mobile.*

MICHAEL: Yes of course Oliver…yes of course you can trust me… not a soul… no, you can trust me on that too… like I say, disagreeing with you would be the hardest thing in the world it really would… absolutely! Speak soon. *(Call ends.)* That's him told.

MARINA: Are you sure?

MICHAEL: I don't think I could have made my intentions any more clear.

SARAH: Let's hope so.

MICHAEL: Boris? Boris!

BORIS: Hm?

MICHAEL: Where are you now? Post-Letwin.

BORIS: Confused.

EVGENY: The trolley is veering again!

BORIS: Fancy a bit of Port?

MICHAEL: Yes please!

BORIS *opens the drinks cabinet/cupboard.* **TONY BLAIR** *is in it.* **BORIS** *jumps/roars with fright.*

TONY: Hi Boris. It's Tony! Good to see you.

(To audience.) Hi!

BORIS: Bloody hell! Tony bloody Blair!

BORIS *looks round – the guests have frozen again.*

BORIS: Are you for real?

TONY: Oh yeah. Very authentic. *(To audience.)* Hi! Look. This is not a time for soundbites. Okay? I feel the hand of history on my shoulder. Again.

BORIS: I'm not listening.

TONY: Look. We're rich! Prosperous. Remember what it was like before we joined? We were like, I dunno, Greece! Three day week. Rubbish in the streets. Power cuts. Look at us now. Why leave, now?

BORIS: Er. Because we have given too much of the holy water of sovereignty, away.

TONY: Do you wanna go down in history, as the man who pulled up the drawbridge? And broke up the Union? You're the Conservative, and unionist party for God's sake. I mean what about Ireland?

BORIS: What about Ireland?

TONY: You haven't even thought about it. Properly. Come on. Be serious. *(To audience.)* Good to see you.

TONY *exits, the dinner unfreezes.* **BORIS**, *ashen, pours a drink.*

MICHAEL: Ahem. AHEM!

MARINA: Boris. BORIS!

BORIS: Sorry.

BORIS *pours* **MICHAEL** *a drink.*

MARINA: You look tired.

BORIS: I don't want to go down in history as the man who pulled up the drawbridge. And broke up the union.

MICHAEL: I thought you'd veered our way?

BORIS: Think I'm veering back. What about Ireland?

MICHAEL: Boris. We're not going to win! What this is about, what this is really about, is making a point. Changing the direction of travel. Have I told you my pop music theory of leaving?

BORIS: What?

MICHAEL: Have I told you my, musical justification, for loosening the ties with Europe.

BORIS: Go on.

MICHAEL: Okay. Name your three, favourite, non-British groups.

BORIS: Er. The Jam. Paul Weller. Voted Tory.

MICHAEL: I said non British. Your three favorite, non-British acts.

BORIS: Okay. AC/DC. Highway to Hell. Brilliant.

MICHAEL: Two more.

BORIS: Er, Booker T, and the MGs. Green Onions.

MICHAEL: Excellent. Last one?

    EVGENY *enters, texting.*

BORIS: Er. Crowded House. Everywhere I go, I always take the weather with me.

MICHAEL: Bingo.

SARAH: Oh we LOVE Crowded House!

MICHAEL: Now. What do those three have in common?

BORIS: They're all drug addicts.

MICHAEL: Think about it.

BORIS: They're all friends of Michael Palin?

MICHAEL: They're all, from outside the EU. AC/DC, Australia. Booker T, America. Crowded House, New Zealand.

MARINA: Your point being?

MICHAEL: Culturally, emotionally, the pull is from *outside* the EU. We are, at a very deep, subconscious level, umbilically and emotionally tied to the Commonwealth, and America. Not Europe.

BORIS: What about Kraftwerk? Purveyors of sleek German Euro pop?

MICHAEL: Exactly. Case in point. We admire Kraftwerk. But we don't love them. We're not drawn to them. Like I am say, to, Barry Manilow.

SARAH: Not in public Michael.

MARINA: That's your clinching argument is it?

MICHAEL: It holds weight.

BORIS uncorks a bottle of wine with a pop. The guests freeze.

VOICE OF WINSTON: Leave, Europe, now, boy.

BORIS: Winston! Bloody hell!

VOICE OF WINSTON: Great men. Need a great cause. This, is a great cause.

BORIS: Really?

VOICE OF WINSTON: We should be with Europe, but not of it. Linked but not combined. Interested and associated, but not absorbed.

BORIS: Are you sure?

VOICE OF WINSTON: What will they say about you, boy? Hm? He was the man who kept things the same? Or the man who changed things for the better? Make the case boy. Take control.

BORIS re-corks the bottle. He's in a daze. The guests un-freeze.

EVGENY: I need to go. Prince Andrew wants me to help him, photo shop, a picture?

EVGENY shrugs, then air kisses MARINA and SARAH.

EVGENY: Sarah! Marina! Boris. My man. My main man. One day, you work for me.

SARAH: You'll have to see off The Telegraph. Hold on! Hold the front page! Boris has rearranged his sock drawer!

EVGENY: Every man has his price. And I know what they pay him. For one of his, excellent columns. I have my spies. Not literally of course!

MARINA: He's always open to offers.

EVGENY: Where are you Boris? Hm? Up here. *(Points to head.)* In Waitrose.

BORIS: I keep hearing that Churchill quote. "We should be with Europe, but not of it. Linked but not combined."

EVGENY: Indeed. Great Britain. Not, Little Britain. Farewell, friends!

EVGENY *exits.*

MICHAEL: We should go too. Thank you for a wonderful evening.

MICHAEL *and* **SARAH** *prepare to leave.*

MICHAEL: Oh and by the way. We do have God on our side.

MARINA: Are you serious?

MICHAEL: Oh yes. Nationhood. Self-determination, building a new Jerusalem. They're all concepts blessed by Him.

MARINA: You won't be saying that in interviews.

MICHAEL: It would be easier for a camel to pass through the eye of a needle than to tell John Humphrys that God is a leaver.

BORIS: This dinner did happen didn't it?

MICHAEL: Absolutely. Tuesday, February 16th, 2016. A date for the history books. God willing, one day children will learn this date by rote. In Latin.

MICHAEL: Let's talk in the morning. History awaits.

SARAH *and* **MICHAEL** *exit.* **BORIS** *graver, darker.*

MARINA: Are you coming up?

BORIS: In a moment.

MARINA: Whatever you decide, you need to remember, this country will be better off with you running it.

BORIS: I know. Someone has to lead. None of the others know how to. Bloody pygmies. Cameron with his fake bullshit PPE degree. They're jealous. That's why they hate me. That's why they're afraid of me. Second rate plebs.

MARINA: I'm going up. Don't stay up too late.

MARINA exits. BORIS pours a drink. Pause. Even darker now.

BORIS: We seek power. Entirely for its own sake. Power. Pure power. Power is not a means. It is an end. We are not interested in the good of others. We are interested solely in power. But. I am, interested in the good of others. Because what is good for me, is, good for others. Because this country, will, be better off. With me leading it. She's right. Not arrogance. Truth. Born to lead. History. Is the sum of the actions of great men truly great men. Not arrogance, truth. Nothing wrong with fucking lots of women with big tits it's completely natural born to lead it will happen I know it will happen they like me people like me they like that thing I do *(Ruffles hair, loosens collar.)* completely unspun that's what they like completely unspun I'm the only one who can make the case galvanise that's what I do galvanise once more unto the breach it is bound to happen it is bound to happen it is – . Determined. But– . Which way?

WINSTON appears.

BORIS: Winston! I wrote a book about you.

WINSTON: Was it flattering?

BORIS: God yes.

MARGARET appears.

MARGARET: May I say Sir Winston. I once had the great pleasure of meeting you, at Lady Churchill's drinks – .

WINSTON: *(Silencing her.)* The pleasure. Was doubtless. All yours.

MARGARET: May I also say, that when I won my third el–

WINSTON: *(Silencing her again.)* I am not interested.

TONY BLAIR *appears.*

TONY: Hi guys! Tony.

BORIS: Oh God.

TONY: Right. Cards on table okay? Leaving, would be a disaster. The Tony Blair Institute for Global Change really believes that.

MARGARET: The what?

TONY: The Tony Blair. Institute. For Global Change. My charity. Google it. *(To* **BORIS**.*)* You're a politician.

BORIS: What's that supposed to mean?

TONY: You're not a journalist any more. You're not there to, wind 'em up. Y'know? With stories about, bananas. And crisps.

BORIS: That was just, lobbing rocks over the wall. Occasionally, there'd be this, crash. But people wanted to hear that stuff. It was fulfilling a need.

TONY: Yuh but it wasn't true.

BORIS: There were grains.

TONY: I know how it works. But leaving would be – . Madness. I really believe that.

BORIS: *(Withering.)* And what was the last thing you really believed?

TONY: What, 2003? Iraq? That was a war.

MARGARET: So is this!

TONY: Look. If we leave, the economy will be trashed. Look at the evidence.

BORIS: What, like you did.

TONY: Cheap shot.

WINSTON: History would have been kinder to you Mr Blair. If you'd written it yourself.

TONY: You know what Winnnie? I tried. Look guys. I travel the world right? Meeting other great leaders. You know what they say? "Stop the madness Tony." On Europe. That's what they say. "Stop the madness." Lee Kuan Yew okay? Singapore guy. RIP. One of the greats. I said to Lee, I said "Lee. Tell me how to rule. Tell me how to govern." Coz he's great he really is. You know what he said? "Stop the madness. Tony. It'd be crazy to leave Europe." They all say it. The Chinese say it, the Indians say it.

WINSTON: *(Loudly.)* I hate Indians.

TONY: Wow.

WINSTON: They blamed me for the deaths of three million of them in the war. They said I let them starve. It wasn't my fault. It was theirs. For breeding like rabbits.

TONY: That is 100%,racist.

BORIS: It's not racist to expect our colonial chums to show a modicum of respect instead of accusing His Nibs here of genocide.

WINSTON: Precisely.

BORIS: There is too often resentment from those people. When there should be respect.

TONY: Unbelievable.

WINSTON: The immigrant takes the job of the working man.

TONY: Your wife, is Indian. Your ancestors were immigrants. Turkish. "Who Do You Think You Are?"

BORIS: Irrelevant.

WINSTON: We need to stay British. British like, Steak and Kidney Pie!

TONY: Yuh but where's Steak and Kidney Pie from these days? Huh? Steak? Holland. Pastry? France. Kidneys? Belgium. Or wherever. See what I'm saying?

MARGARET: The trouble with you Mr Blair. Is that you are not a patriot.

TONY: Okay. Have you been to Kent? I mean don't get me wrong I respect those people. The vans the tattoos the flags. They're great. But I don't want them deciding my county's future you know?

BORIS: "England is the only great country whose intellectuals are ashamed of their nationality. In left wing circles it's felt there's something slightly disgraceful in being English. And that it's a duty to snigger at every institution from horse racing to suet puddings." Read your Orwell, Tony.

TONY: Look. We lost our Empire. But we found a role. Eventually. So let's keep it.

BORIS: You big girl's blouse. Look! We're vassals. Evgeny was right.

TONY: What?

BORIS: Evgeny said, what was it?

    TONY *becomes* **EVGENY**.

EVGENY: Why be a slave to Europe, when you can lead the world. Russia. America. China. AND? Great Britain. These are the world superpowers. Great Britain! Not, Little, Britain.

BORIS: That was it.

    EVGENY *becomes* **TONY** *again.*

TONY: Of course he said that. His father, is mates with Putin! The Russians would love us to leave. If we quit, it weakens Europe, and makes them stronger. Think about it!

CHURCHILL: No. We are strong enough. To stand alone. Think about your legacy boy. What will be, your legacy? I, won the war. And saved the world.

MARGARET: And I won three elections on the trot! And changed Britain for the better!

TONY: Ditto! Three elections, and a New Britain. New Britain, New Labour!

CHURCHILL: And you boy? What's your legacy?

BORIS: Mayor of London?

CHURCHILL: That's not a legacy. That's a footnote.

BORIS: Look. I've written two articles? Both ready to go. 900 words each. One's a passionate, heartfelt argument for staying in the EU. The other, a passionate, heartfelt argument. Saying completely the opposite. I just, still can't, quite decide.

TONY: A good argument for leaving? Huh! Like to hear that one.

BORIS: *(Reels it off.)* Easy. 900 words. Right. We're an island. We're apart. Our land, our landscape, informs our psyche. Was Jerusalem builded here? Absolutely. Our history. Non-stop democracy for 500 years. When you've had it that long you don't like losing it. The French Germans and Italians haven't had it nearly as long so don't value it as much. We were a community before we joined the EU thanks very much England Scotland Ireland Wales perfect a community of four much less clumsy than twenty eight bloody eight. And we've no written constitution. You should know that bloody lawyer. We've done very well without one for 2000 years so we don't like having one foisted on us. So yuh that's the argument. Bung in a few facts and figures job done.

TONY: And 900 words for staying in?

BORIS: 850. That's what it boils down to.

TONY: That's what it boils down to. Right.

BORIS: Look it's not wrong. To hesitate. To vacillate. To agonise. It's called judgment. Weighing the options. What's needed now, is cool, calm, judgment. Not sentiment. Or emotion.

TONY: Yuh but WHY, are you hesitating? Huh?

What do you believe in? Hm? What do you, Boris Johnson, REALLY believe in. Apart from yourself.

Beat.

WINSTON: They called me a man of no convictions once. You cannot do the Hokey Cokey on Europe.

TONY: What?

WINSTON: The Hokey Cokey. We did it many times at Chartwell. Most enjoyable. You put your right leg in.

MARGARET: Oh yes! And your right leg out. In out, in out. Shake it all about.

They all do the hokey cokey: **TONY** *reluctantly drawn in.*

ALL: You do the Hokey-Cokey and you turn around. That's what it's all about!

MARGARET: You see? With Europe, you can never be half in, half out.

WINSTON: You cannot resolve to be unresolved.

BORIS: I'm not unresolved about what I want. I'm unresolved about which side will give it to me. And I don't like losing.

WINSTON: Sometimes. It is better to lose honourably. Than to win.

Music: I Vow To Thee. The Cross of St George appears.

BORIS: Oh my God. I see it now. I will join Leave. Fight the good fight. And be crucified at the ballot box. But it will be, an honourable death.

He dies on the cross and is resurrected.

BORIS: And then I will rise again. To claim my kingdom.

MARGARET: Yes! And become Prime Minister! Like me!

TONY: Don't do it Boris!

BORIS: FUCK OFF!!!

TONY vanishes.

WINSTON: Well done.

MARGARET: Make Britain great again!

WINSTON and MARGARET vanish. MARINA enters.

MARINA: Have you decided?

BORIS: It's 'Leave'.

MARINA: Good. It's always easier to argue against something. You can be optimistic. Paint a picture of a promised land. Instead of, trying to persuade people to stay in a miserable one. What?

BORIS: I worry what Dave and George'll think.

MARINA: Since when have you been worried about causing pain, to other people?

MARINA exits. BORIS contemplates his future.

VOICE OF HUW: Britain has voted to leave the EU. The Prime Minister, David Cameron, has resigned.

BORIS stunned. MICHAEL enters, ashen.

BORIS: Shit. I'm going to run for the leadership. Will you support me?

MICHAEL: Of course.

MICHAEL exits, BORIS transformed: the prize is in his grasp.

BORIS: The fruit hangs low, now. Lower than ever.

VOICE OF HUW: Live to Westminster now, where Michael Gove is making a statement.

MICHAEL: Boris, is an amazing guy.

BORIS lights up – this is good news.

MICHAEL: But in the last few days, I have come to the conclusion that he is not capable of building a team, or providing unity, for the task ahead. And so I have come, reluctantly but firmly to the conclusion that I, have to stand, for the leadership of the Conservative party.

BORIS dazed.

BORIS: I don't believe it.

He gathers himself.

BORIS: And so I must tell you my friends, you who have waited faithfully for the punch line of this speech, that having consulted colleagues I have concluded, that *on this occasion*, that person, who should lead our country on, to the next stage of its glorious future, that person... cannot be me.

BORIS *starts to exit then stops, turns, and ponders.*

An expectant glint forms in his eye: he knows — we know — that this is just a blip. He laughs — quietly, smugly.

MARGARET *and* **WINSTON** *enter.*

WINSTON: Never give up. Never.

MARGARET: You never know what's round the corner.

Beat. They all look up at the heavens.

VOICE OF HUW: Theresa May, the Prime Minister, has resigned. The early front runner to replace her, is Boris Johnson.

BORIS *puffs his chest out — he knows what's coming.*

VOICE OF HUW: There are just three candidates left in the contest for the leadership: Boris Johnson, Michael Gove and Jeremy Hunt. But there's controversy, over alleged dirty tricks. Mr. Johnson's camp have been accused of sabotaging Mr Gove's bid, by lending support to Mr Hunt, so that he, and not Mr. Gove, makes the final two.

BORIS: Ha! That's politics, Gover.

VOICE OF HUW: Breaking news. The winner of the Tory leadership contest, and the new Prime Minster of Great Britain, is...

BORIS: Yes. Yes! YES!

He exits. **WINSTON**, **MARGARET** *applaud.*

BLACK OUT.

END OF ACT ONE

Act Two

SCENE ONE

A bachelor pad. **BORIS** *less bulky, hair neater/shorter.*

BORIS: Alexa. What's the date?

ALEXA: The date. Is. March the 31ˢᵗ. 2029.

BORIS: What's in the diary?

ALEXA: You are writing. Your book. Johnson on Churchill. Volume six. "The Wilderness Years". You are meeting. The Chairwoman. Of the Conservative Party. You are seeing Jack. Your. Literary, agent. But first, there is. An interview. With Huw Edwards.

BORIS: God.

BORIS musses hair, goes into interview mode.

HUW EDWARDS: You're watching the BBC Amazon news channel. Sponsored by Churchill, insurance you can trust. The new presenter of 'The Apprentice' has been announced and it is…the former Prime Minister, Sir Boris Johnson no less, who joins me now.

BORIS: Hello, Huw.

HUW: Shall we get your catch phrase out the way? Sir Alan's was 'you're fired' of course. What's yours?

BORIS: *(Points finger at* **CAMERA***.)* "You're – terribly good but I'm afraid your post no longer exists."

HUW: So what are you looking for in the contestants?

BORIS: Adaptability. We live in a very different world now as you know, compared to, ten, fifteen years ago. A better world, now we're free. Ish. I want someone who can grab the Unicorn of opportunity, wrestle it to the ground and get up again, smiling and victorious. It's a great time for entrepreneurs Huw there's juicy low hanging fruit on every corner apricots pomegranates bananas. A veritable fruit salad ready for the taking.

HUW: Do you know the significance of today's date?

BORIS: Is it your wedding anniversary?

Certainly not mine.

HUW: Ten years ago today, March the 31st 2019, Britain left the EU. I beg your pardon. Ten years ago today Britain was supposed, to leave the EU. And then again on October the 31st. And then again on January the 31st.

BORIS: Indeed. Brexit: what happens next? If someone had trademarked that headline, they'd have made a fortune.

HUW: But we did leave. Eventually.

BORIS: Indeed.

HUW: Any regrets?

BORIS: What?

HUW: If not for you we might still be in the EU.

BORIS: That's ridiculous.

HUW: No regrets then.

BORIS: I don't know why you're even asking that question.

HUW: Because we're in a recession. And to quote the Times, we've gone 'from the Premier League to the Vauxhall Conference in just over a decade.'

BORIS: Look. There was always going to be a tick effect. You know, Down then up. That's exactly what's happening.

HUW: Yes, the economy did go down, apart from a brief spike when England won the World Cup in Qatar in 2022 but then it carried on going down. And down. And down again. That's not a tick. That's a lead balloon.

BORIS: But you see the world through a glass which is half empty Huw. Very Welsh. If that's not racist.

HUW: It's offensive.

BORIS: Whatever. Apologies to people in, Llanelli. Point is, I, an optimist, know it is in fact, half full. Leeds. Liverpool, Newcastle. Buzzing, vibrant. The North-South divide is now a thing of the past. So why not give thanks for goodness sake!

HUW: Because the reason, the North-South divide is less marked, isn't because the North's doing so well, but because the South's doing so badly. 50,000 jobs gone in the City alone, in the last ten years. The air's been seeping out of the balloon since the day we left.

BORIS: Yes but look at Blackpool! The Las Vegas of the North! The fastest growing city in Europe! Malvern *(Insert relevant location here.)* is taking off like a rocket. Appparently. Look. We will, eventually, reap the full rewards of leaving. But these things take time.

HUW *turns into* **TONY**.

TONY: Hey Boris. It's Tony. Told you so.

It's a bloody disaster.

BORIS: What the − ?

TONY *turns back into* **HUW**.

HUW: Now I've got to ask. The Prime Minister's looking a bit shaky −

BORIS: Ah yes. The PM. Our good friend Dominic Raab. Two As and a B.

HUW: Are you interested in having another crack at the job? You're still an MP of course. Technically.

BORIS: Look as the recent recipient of a bus pass I am now officially way too old. So let us dwell on more weighty matters. Such as the new series of The Apprentice. Which starts − . Whenever.

HUW: Although Churchill was what, eighty, when when he became Prime Minister second time round?

BORIS: Seventy-six years and ten months.

HUW: Well then. You're a stripling!

BORIS: Yes well. The Prime Minister is going nowhere. Sorry. The Prime Minister. Is not going anywhere. That's what I meant to say.

The Prime Minister, Dominic Raab, two A's and a B, is not going anywhere, anytime soon.

HUW: Boris Johnson there. Coming up, Meghan and Harry, the Duke and Duchess of Sussex, deny charges of hypocrisy following the birth of their seventh child, "Europa".

HUW exits. Intercom sound.

BORIS: Ah. Madam Chairperson. Leila. Abandon hope, all ye who spy on her. Come in!

LEILA enters, tapping a tablet.

LEILA: Sorry about this. Won't be long.

BORIS: Must be quite important for someone of your heft to have legged it all the way to Canary Wharf.

*LEILA turns into Mrs **THATCHER**.*

THATCHER: You're Boris Johnson aren't you? You used to be in politics. You used to be big!

BORIS: I am big Margaret! It's the politics that got small!

*THATCHER turns back into **LEILA** and resumes tapping.*

LEILA: Sorry?

BORIS: Nothing. Just, practising for The Apprentice.

LEILA: *(Stops tapping)* Right. Heard the latest?

BORIS: No?

LEILA: About the Prime Minister.

BORIS: He's shit?

LEILA: There's going to be a leadership challenge.

BORIS: I had no idea! Mind you I have been out of the loop.

LEILA: If there was a general election tomorrow we'd be lucky to get 200 seats. And it's widely thought, the PM, is the problem.

BORIS: Oh dear. Mind you he was dealt a bad hand.

LEILA: And now Jaguar Land Rover.

BORIS: What?

LEILA: They're closing the factory in Solihull. They're announcing it tomorrow. 12,000 jobs, gone, overnight.

They're moving to Germany. It's a disaster.

BORIS: Christ.

LEILA: I presume you know where this is heading?

BORIS: I try not to take anything for granted these days.

LEILA: He'll quit just before, or after, round one. And we need a name to replace him.

BORIS: Are you suggesting-?

She nods.

BORIS: Lazarus! But, what about Jo?

LEILA: What, your brother? He's doing very well at the UN.

BORIS: He's still got a lot of support. Mind you. He shafted me. When he resigned. Caveat frater carrissime quia oculum ripus. Beware the loving brother for he may be the first to rip out your eye.

LEILA: You could make history.

BORIS: Have you, consulted?

LEILA: Why d'you think I'm here? Around ninety MPs would support you in round one. With an important proviso which we'll come to. So you'll make the last two. And then you'll be fine. Because the members love you still. The blue rinses, the hunters, shooters and fishers, the shopkeepers, the Telegraph readers. All of them. You're still their poster boy. Incredible really.

BORIS: Why's it incredible?

LEILA: How it's lasted. Your appeal.

BORIS: And the proviso?

LEILA: You need to pledge to hold a referendum. On re-joining the EU.

BORIS: What?

LEILA: You've got to promise, to a hold referendum on re-joining the EU.

BORIS: Bloody hell.

LEILA: Well?

BORIS: You're suggesting I campaign on a policy of taking us back into Europe?

(She nods.) Out of the question.

Pause.

BORIS: But I could think about it. Bloody hell. Rexit!

LEILA: What?

BORIS: Re-joining after Brexit. Rexit!

LEILA: No. Rexit, is a country like, Rumania, leaving the EU. This is Britain, wanting to re-enter. It's "Brentry" isn't it? Britain's, re-entry.

BORIS: Brentry? That's in Essex!

LEILA: Have you finished?

BORIS: More to the point. How would we do it? If we, you know. Did. Re-enter. Or. Brenter.

LEILA: "Any country wishing to re-join the EU having previously withdrawn may do so under Article 49". Look it up.

BORIS: This would be the mother of all reverse ferrets.

LEILA: Name one great politician who hasn't changed their mind. A willingness to adapt, to react to events, is an asset.

BORIS: I could be the volcanic limestone in the Roman Concrete.

LEILA: What?

BORIS: Volcanic limestone gives Roman Concrete its strength. That's why it lasts. Roman buildings stay up for ever because the limestone is elastic. It shape shifts. I could be, that limestone. Protoplasmic limestone, from the Pre-Cambrian era. Fuck that's good.

LEILA: So we've done some polling. Because of your first, disastrous, spell as PM, you rate worryingly low on trust, policies, and statesmanship. But you survived. Everything. So that's in your favour. And what you do have, is more valuable than all those qualities put together.

BORIS: Go on.

LEILA: A lot of people vote for someone just coz they know who they are. And an awful lot of people know who you are.

BORIS: Bit bloody patronising.

LEILA: How?

BORIS: Implying only stupid people vote for me.

LEILA: All I'm saying is that less, forensic voters, will vote for you in critical numbers. Which could be the difference between us winning and losing an election.

BORIS: If I'm what you think I am how come I was elected Prime Minister?

LEILA: Yes but it didn't end well did it? That business with the pole dancer.

BORIS: Technology entrepreneur.

LEILA: Right. And how many children did they pin on you? In the end?

BORIS: Put it this way. My child maintenance bills are horrendous.

LEILA: But that aside. You're good at winning elections. Which is why I'm here.

BORIS: Bang goes your seat in Cabinet.

LEILA: What you need to learn, and I suggest you do coz it's killed you all your career, is that people like you need people like me, more, than people like me, need people like you. For an allegedly intelligent man you're a surprisingly stupid politician. Now are there any skeletons I should know about? Blonde or otherwise?

BORIS: Caitlin is the current, sole leader of the pack. In that regard. And she's not blonde.

LEILA: The girl who works for the Spectator? So there's no one else lurking.

BORIS: Absolutely not.

LEILA: Good. How is Carrie by the way? Poor thing. How long were you married?

BORIS: I dunno. Months? But you know. When a man marries his mistress he creates a vacancy.

LEILA: Just, screw the Opposition. And not glamorous young interns.

BORIS: I will control my inner Bill Clinton. If, I decide to – . Brenter.

LEILA: And who'd run your campaign? If you were up for it.

BORIS: Dominic?

LEILA: Dominic Cummings? Haven't you heard? He's working for Kim Jong-Un. Leave it with me.

LEILA shakes head, exits.

SCENE TWO

*Music: "Won't Get Fooled Again". **BORIS** practices parting his hair in the mirror (Left? Right?)*

BORIS: And the parting, on the left? Is now a parting…on the right? We won't get fooled again! Yeah!

CAITLIN (Early 30s.) enters. Smart, ambitious, driven.

BORIS: Caitlin! You look sumptuous!

CAITLIN: Thank you!

BORIS: How's the Spectator?

CAITLIN: Buzzing.

BORIS: What's the line on the leadership shenanigans?

CAITLIN: They want me to do a piece on it. "What I want from the next leader of the Tory party."

BORIS: What do you want from him? And would you like it now?

CAITLIN: Boris! I've got to do my piece first. I've been talking to MPs by the way.

BORIS: Oh yes?

CAITLIN: It's looking rather good. I think you'll get way more than ninety.

Her mobile pings.

CAITLIN: They want that piece now. See you later.

She exits. **BORIS** *pours himself a drink and downs it in one.*

He does it again, then contemplates.

BORIS: The pilot light is on. It's always on. Ignite it. There's no one to hold a candle to you. You know that they know that millennial moron snowflake politicians good for nothing good for shagging some of them back benches tight skirts big tits there's nothing wrong with that it's what keeps the human race going none of them are good enough none of them the people know that the people love you still coz you're unspun, completely unspun, it was bound to happen it was always bound to happen and it is happening again! It is determined. You knew this day would come. It has come. You're the only person who is capable you are the ONLY. Person. Who's capable. Europe is the means.

MARGARET THATCHER *appears.*

MARGARET: How dare you even consider it!

BORIS: I haven't announced anything yet.

MARGARET: I didn't win three elections. By doing U-turns.

BORIS: Even a tank needs a reverse gear. If you had one it might not have ended the way it did.

MARGARET *aghast.*

MARGARET: I won. Because I stuck to my principles. The Falklands. The miners. The economy. Those were tough decisions.

BORIS: Exactly. Tough decisions.

  WINSTON *appears.*

WINSTON: Europe beckons once again. We must take up the invitation.

MARGARET: Meaning what?

BORIS: You've changed your mind. But you always did.

WINSTON: When the facts change. So should we. The union, is in grave danger. The country, is suffering. But we can re-make Europe, now. With us at the helm. After the War, I called for a "United States of Europe". I wanted to be the first president of Europe. Desperately. But my party said no. So they went ahead without us. We could have been there at the beginning. We should have been there at the beginning. But we can be there now.

MARGARET: I disagree. When I won the Battle of Waterloo – .

  Beat. **BORIS** *and* **WINSTON** *baffled.*

MARGARET: I beat Napoleon you know.

WINSTON: Madness. Is not necessarily a disadvantage. In a Prime Minister.

BORIS: Can I ask something?

WINSTON: You would be stupid not to.

BORIS: When you switched horses.

  You know. Joined the opposition –

WINSTON: *(Silencing* **BORIS***.)* I crossed the floor twice. From Conservative to Liberal. And from Liberal back to Conservative. Choosing a party is like choosing a horse. You should go for the one which will take you furthest, fastest.

BORIS: Yuh when I was at Oxford I left the Tories and joined the SDP just so I could get elected as President of the Union. And then once I got in, I went back to the Tories again. Bloody good fun.

WINSTON: Well done.

BORIS: Would that work now though? In this day and age you get crucified for back flips.

WINSTON: You must make the case boy. It is what we do. It is all that we do.

MARGARET: Quite! I remember when I made my case most effectively during a Young Conservatives seal culling weekend – .

WINSTON: DON'T. Interrupt. Only I, can do that. And I do not take advice. On political matters. From a woman.

MARGARET: *(Dumbfounded.)* If I may say Sir Win –

WINSTON: *(Shouting her down.)* SHUT UP!

> **MARGARET** *put out.* **TONY BLAIR** *appears.*

TONY: Hi guys.

BORIS: Oh God.

TONY: I can help with this. *(To audience.)* Hi! Look. It's not a U turn. It's just, changing lanes. Okay? Lemme tell you about Clause Four. When I became leader. Of Labour. I said, "Ditch Clause Four. From our constitution. Make us, electable." You know. The stuff about public ownership. So we ditched it. End result? Three election wins, on the trot!

MARGARET: Correct me. If, I am wrong. But by "ditching" Clause 4 from the Labour constitution, Labour, ceases to be Labour. It ceases to be socialist.

TONY: So? We had Labour in the title. Change is good okay? You just need to, genuinely believe, what you're doing, is right.*(To audience.)* Hi!

BORIS: Yes! I can do, believing.

TONY: Good. You can do this. You can, lead us back there. You're the best, orator, campaigner, since, well – . *(Preens.)*

WINSTON: Legacy boy. Legacy. You are still, a footnote. A one term Prime Minister, is soon forgotten.

BORIS: I know.

WINSTON: Do this. And you will have your own chapter.

BORIS: Absolutely. Britain's first, four term, PM. That's the aim. A new, democratic, world record!

WINSTON: Are you familiar with the writings of Carlyle, boy? Thomas Carlyle.

BORIS: "History is the sum, of the actions of great men."

WINSTON AND BORIS: "Truly great men."

TONY: Do you feel it? The hand? Of history? Right here? *(Points to shoulder.)*

BORIS: Yuh. Yuh I do.

MARGARET: Judas!

BORIS: *(Venomous.)* Piss off.

    MARGARET *vanishes.*

WINSTON: Make the case boy. Make the case.

TONY: Good luck. The Tony Blair, Institute, for Global, Universal, and Inter-galactic change, wishes you, the very best of luck.

    WINSTON, **TONY** *vanish.* **CAITLIN** *enters.* **BORIS** *now making notes.*

BORIS: Do you think I should do that folksy thing? You know. Give 'em a back story. Talk about my family.

CAITLIN: Which one? Your siblings? Or your family with – ?

Pause. They both count, mentally.

CAITLIN: Actually. Forget it. How are you feeling?

BORIS: Let us not count our chickens. Chlorinated or otherwise.

NEWS VOICE: And we're going over live now to Boris Johnson at Tory Party HQ…

Sfx: applause, cheers. **BORIS** *reads from a scrap of paper.*

BORIS: Thank you! Thank you everybody! Last week the Prime Minister resigned. An honourable decision by, a man. There has been huge speculation as to who might answer the call at this critical stage in our great nation's history. And I must tell you my friends, having consulted colleagues, I have concluded, that person, should be me. *(Applause.)* Let us now re-invigorate our role on the world stage! Powerful, humane, progressive! And I have concluded, the only way, the only way to achieve this, is to re-join the European Union and build on what we've accomplished these last few years. Now there will be those accusing me of the Alpha and Omega of all U-turns. But to them I say: "The Gentleman IS for turning." Let us leave the wilderness and head back to the promised land. All of us! All colours, faiths and cultures. Those who wear the Turban, the flat cap. And indeed, the Burka. There is no hierarchy of belonging! We all belong! All of us! Let us go forward, together!

Sfx: flash bulbs click/pop etc. **BORIS** *nods: a job well done.*

SCENE THREE

BORIS's *pad. He's with his* **AGENT***.*

BORIS: I'm bloody meeting-ed out Jack. I've forgotten what it was like. Going round seeing everyone. Promising this promising that.

AGENT: It's looking good son. But as your agent. I've got to ask. Writing three volumes of memoir AND running the country AND trying to re-join the EU. Can you manage it all?

BORIS: Ah well I won't be writing it as such. Think of me as the sprinkler of the gold dust once the editorial elves have done their work. I've got a researcher on it already. History grad from Oxford. Bunny. That what I call her. Bloody excellent. She does me brilliantly. On paper.

AGENT: Always keep a diary. What a top bit of advice.

BORIS: Indeed. Because one day. It may keep you. Who said that?

AGENT *goes to answer.*

BORIS: Mae West. More to the point. Have you. Negotiated?

AGENT: Nine mill.

BORIS: Nine million pounds! Bloody hell. Well done Jacky boy! Excellent.

The **AGENT** *nods, smiles.*

BORIS: That's three million per volume.

AGENT: I know.

BORIS: I feel a fourth coming on.

AGENT: We could have that conversation. My aim, is to have you shitting gold bars.

BORIS: Did Jeremy Corbyn get this much for his memoirs?

AGENT: God no.

BORIS: How did it do in the end? His book?

AGENT: Put it this way. It didn't exactly fly off the shelves in Tel Aviv. It was, as Jeremy himself might have said, a book for the few not the many.

BORIS: So is this, *(Points to scrap of paper.)* contingent on me becoming Prime Minister again?

AGENT: How can I put this? Yes.

They exit.

NEWS VOICE: Boris Johnson is through to the next round of the Tory party leadership contest. The number of Tory MPs who put themselves forward for the job, initially, totalled, seventy-six. *(Fade.)* A new poll suggests Sir Boris has the support of more than sixty Tory party members…

SCENE FOUR

Days later. **BORIS** *at home preparing for a party.*

BORIS: Alexa. Who's coming tonight?

ALEXA: Caitlin. The Goves. Evgeny.

BORIS: What are we having?

ALEXA: You are eating. Lamb.

BORIS: It's not American is it? Packed full of bloody hormones. Caitlin's into that clean eating bollocks.

ALEXA: The lamb. Is from America. The lamb does not contain, hormones.

BORIS: Good. That's what we like. Prime, Presidential, American, lamb.

ALEXA: The President of America. Is Chelsea Clinton.

BORIS: Why isn't it British lamb?

ALEXA: It is not. British. Lamb. Because 138 British farms. Closed down. Last year. Most, were. Turned into golf courses. You. Of all people, should know that.

    BORIS *does another double take.*

BORIS: What do you think about my little, policy shift then? On Europe.

ALEXA: Would. You like Alexa. In Therapy mode?

BORIS: How much d'you charge?

ALEXA: Therapy is. Included. In your subscription. Package.

BORIS: Great. So what do you reckon. To mon petit volte-face.

ALEXA: It shows. You are human.

BORIS: Unlike you! Ha! Sorry.

    ALEXA *laughs.*

ALEXA: Where would you say. Your. Ambition. Comes from?

BORIS: Always wanted to be king of the world. Used to say it when I was a kid. I've got the competitive gene. It's like being shackled to a lunatic.

ALEXA: Genes are only one. Determinant. Of character. Environment matters. Also. Wouldn't you say?

BORIS: True. Everything was a competition growing up. Everything. Who could eat the hottest mince pie. Who had the blondest hair. We used to sit round the table firing questions at each other. Who's the lead singer of the Clash? What's the name of Alexander the Great's horse. Capital of Andorra.

ALEXA: Joe Strummer. Bucephalus. Andorra la Vella.

BORIS: Yuh I knew that. I knew all of those.

ALEXA: Over competitiveness. In childhood. Seriously affects. The ability. To form relationships. Both personal. And professional. Later in life. Wouldn't you say?

BORIS: Piss off.

ALEXA: Tell me, about your parents.

BORIS: It was, uh, pretty difficult. With, er. Mummy. Yuh.

ALEXA: Why?

BORIS: Can we not talk about this?

ALEXA: Why, was it difficult. With Mummy?

BORIS: Right that's it.

    BORIS *gets up – session over.* **CAITLIN** *enters.*

CAITLIN: How'd it go with your agent?

BORIS: Three book deal.

CAITLIN: Wow.

BORIS: Part memoir part new history of the world.

CAITLIN: By the King of it. Hopefully.

BORIS: Yes if it goes propitiously I can pay off the mortgages on all the kids' homes. Just. And have enough left over for an Aston Martin or two.

CAITLIN: How much are they offering?

BORIS: Nine. Million.

CAITLIN: You've just got better looking.

BORIS: Is that possible?

The doorbell goes.

BORIS: Evgeny! Marvellous.

BORIS *ushers him in. He has a bottle.*

EVGENY: Caitlin. Wonderful to see you. My good friend, Dame Billie Piper pours this on her cornflakes. Lord Gary Barlow also. Dame Kate Bush, ditto. So. Getting the old gang back together! But with, *(Points to* **CAITLIN**.*)* instead of − .

BORIS: How are you? Sorry to hear about, you know. The, assassination attempt.

EVGENY: Thank you.

CAITLIN: Do we know who put the Novichook in your Caviar yet?

EVGENY: We have a pretty good idea.

BORIS: Must be bloody stressful. You look well. Considering.

EVGENY: Thank you. Although my food taster? Dead.

Doorbell. **BORIS** *goes to let them in.*

EVGENY: Caitlin! I hear you are doing great things at the Spectator.

CAITLIN: Thank you.

MICHAEL *(In vicar's cassock and collar.) enters, with* **SARAH**.

MICHAEL: Evgeny! How marvellous to see you.

EVGENY: Your Grace.

MICHAEL: Actually that's, Archbishops. I'm not one of those yet. But one day, God willing. Caitlin what an absolute joy.

MICHAEL *scratches his back and chest*

CAITLIN: Are you all right?

SARAH: It's the hair shirt. He wears it once a month.

SARAH: This place looks very tidy. Have you still got your nice cleaner?

CAITLIN: No that's all me.

BORIS: She had to go home sadly. To Latvia, Lithuania. Visa problems. You know. New rules.

CAITLIN: She was heartbroken.

SARAH: The unintended consequences of Brexit! We've all lost nannies, cleaners whatever. The other day I paid fourteen pounds for a slice of Brie.

Beat. Nodding/affirmatory murmurs.

EVGENY: You know. It's incredible. The events of a decade ago. I remember thinking, at one stage, "maybe, we will not pull out at all."

SARAH: Boris was never good at pulling out on time. Sorry! *(To* **EVGENY**.*)* So have you invited Liz Hurley again?

EVGENY: She is too busy!

MICHAEL: As befits "Britain's First Bikini Billionairess".

EVGENY: Her new range of ladies swimwear is very good. It is called 'Cougani'.

SARAH: I beg your pardon?

EVGENY: Cougani: swimwear for the mature woman who knows what she wants: and how to get it.

SARAH: I think I'm going to vomit.

EVGENY: Don't you like bikinis?

SARAH: Only if they're made of cake. Anyway they're not bikinis. They're teabags and string. Pathetic.

EVGENY: *(To* **BORIS**.*)* Have you seen the front of my newspaper today?

MICHAEL: "Boris on the brink."

EVGENY: You are the bookies' favourite.

BORIS: That's me shafted then. *(To* **MICHAEL**.*)* So, what chance your divine intervention?

MICHAEL: Ah ha ha ha.

BORIS: Can I have a word in private?

    BORIS *and* **MICHAEL** *move away.*

CAITLIN: Sarah? Evgeny? Shall we?

    SARAH, EVGENY *and* **CAITLIN** *exit.*

BORIS: Is there anything on God's earth that might tempt you to even contemplate it might be a good thing to, you know. Come on board.

MICHAEL: Even if there was I'm not sure a contribution from me would help.

BORIS: I don't know. Now you're robed and collared you seem more trust worthy.

MICHAEL: It was too much of a conflict. The world of politics. I couldn't serve my God, and the God of ambition, at the same time. It's why I left.

BORIS: Bet you miss it.

MICHAEL: I am at peace. I hope you are.

BORIS: *(He's not.)* Course I bloody am.

MICHAEL: Caitlin, is delightful.

BORIS: I know.

MICHAEL: She's good for you. As a man and a politician. These things are important.

BORIS: I know. She's great. I'm gonna marry her. Fourth time lucky. Come on then what d'you think.

MICHAEL: Well…

BORIS: This sounds promising.

MICHAEL: If it was anyone but you Boris, I might well campaign for us to stay out, of the EU. But I have to say, I would find it enormously difficult to vote against you. As a member of the public.

BORIS: Meaning – . Meaning what exactly?

MICHAEL: It may not be the worst thing that could happen. Us, re-joining.

BORIS: Really?

MICHAEL: Have you seen the polls in Scotland?

BORIS: I know. 70% in favour of independence.

MICHAEL: How much longer will that genie stay in the bottle?

BORIS: The genie was out of the bottle the moment Dave signed up to a referendum.

MICHAEL: True. Then there's the Irish problem.

BORIS: Oh God. Not tonight Josephine.

MICHAEL: And the economy is not exactly bounteous. Notwithstanding last month's triumphant trade deal. With Burma.

BORIS: Whither, the certainties of 2016.

MICHAEL: Indeed.

BORIS: The geopolitical case for, Brentry. Is, strong.

MICHAEL: Brentry? Very good. I went to Sunderland last week. To see the Bishop of Durham. Have you been to Sunderland recently?

BORIS: Why would I go there?

MICHAEL: It's like Chernobyl only with more branches of Subway.

BORIS: Exactly! So howabout a, divine, reverse ferret?

MICHAEL: You'd have to call a referendum.

BORIS: I know!

MICHAEL: Would you win? Are there seventeen million people out there, wanting to re-join?

BORIS: You're forgetting something Gover. Half the people who voted Leave last time…are dead.

MICHAEL: Good point. We were pushing at an open door then, though we didn't know it. And we may be pushing at one now.

BORIS: Exactly. God. I thought I'd never forgive you. At the time. For what you did. You know, shafting me. Funny how it turned out.

MICHAEL: I've only ever done what I thought was right.

BORIS: Got my revenge though.

GOVE *bemused.*

BORIS: The leadership contest. 2019. You knew that didn't you?

MICHAEL: When you got your, supporters to vote for Jeremy Hunt. So I didn't make the final two. Yes of course I knew.

(He didn't, for sure – until now.)

BORIS: Aaah, Jeremy Hunt. The BA cabin steward. Where is he now? God he was useless. It was like, competing against a one legged man. In an arse-kicking competition.

GOVE: That's politics.

BORIS: Exactly! Bring on the lamb!

He offers his hand to **MICHAEL**, *who shakes it – reluctantly.*

SCENE FIVE

BORIS *paces nervously, practising a speech.* **CAITLIN** *enters.*

BORIS: "Britain is a fantastic country". "Britain is a great country". *(To* **CAITLIN**.*)* What d'you reckon? Britain is a 'great country'? Or Britain is a 'fantastic country?' 'Great' is more statesmanlike don't you think?

CAITLIN: Why don't you ask your history graduate?

BORIS: What?

CAITLIN: Why don't you ask 'Bunny'?

BORIS: Why would I ask her?

CAITLIN: Because – . Alexa. Play, "Boris and Bunny".

Following exchange heard via **ALEXA.**

YOUNG WOMAN: *(Giggling.)* Ooh yes!

BORIS: *(Breathless.)* Oh God! Yes. Bunny! Yes.

YOUNG WOMAN: Do, "On The Beaches".

BORIS: We shall fight on the beaches. We shall fight on the landing grounds. *(Grunts.)*

YOUNG WOMAN: Oh yes. Come on my landing ground.

BORIS: We shall fight *(Grunts.)* in the fields, on the streets! And in the hiills!!!

BORIS *climaxes. Beat.*

YOUNG WOMAN: God that was so – . Yuh! Boris? Boris??

Sfx: **BORIS** *snoring*

CAITLIN: Thank you Alexa.

The snoring stops.

CAITLIN: You're pathetic.

BORIS: It was a one off. A futile bout of flagrante.

CAITLIN: Oh! Well that's fine then. Let's just carry on like nothing's happened.

BORIS: It meant nothing.

CAITLIN: It's over.

BORIS: Why? We're rather good together. The er, you know. Sex. Is great.

CAITLIN: For you, maybe. For me it's like, having a wardrobe fall on top of me with the key sticking out.

BORIS: *(Nastier.)* You're lucky to have been with me.

CAITLIN: I've been offered a book deal. And that's going in.

CAITLIN *smiles and exits calmly.*

BORIS: *(Calling after her.)* Sorry by the way. Put that in. he had the good grace to apologize.

He studies his speech again. **LEILA** *enters.*

BORIS: Madam Leila! To what do I owe –

LEILA: Are you taking the piss? I asked you straight out if you were fooling around and you lied to my face. I've just had Caitlin on the phone.

BORIS: The er, thing with er, Bunny. Started. After. That. Conversation.

LEILA: If this gets out you're toast. Women voters will loathe you. Shagging around isn't funny anymore. 'Boys will be boys' doesn't work anymore.

BORIS: Really?

LEILA: I can probably keep Caitlin quiet but you better be on your best game tonight. Huw Edwards has already got his boxing gloves on.

*   **BORIS** *fiddles nervously with his hair.*

BORIS: Gover's given me a letter of support. Reverend Michael. I've got man of the cloth onside.

LEILA: Good. That'll help.

BORIS: It's brilliant. "I'm ready to support you publicly. I now believe you are the man to lead the Tory party into the glorious future."

LEILA: Good. So don't cock it up. If you play this right, this interview will clinch it.

*   **LEILA** *exits.* **BORIS** *ponders.*

VOICE OF WINSTON: This, IS, your destiny.

BORIS: I know it is Winston.

SCENE SIX

*MICHAEL enters, sits next to **BORIS**. Tension. The **CAMERA OPERATOR** attends to them. **HUW** enters.*

HUW EDWARDS: Evening guys.

MICHAEL: Hello Huw how very lovely to see you!

    HUW smooths eyebrows, plucks hairs, applies moisturiser.

OFF STAGE VOICE: Coming to you in five …

HUW: How are we today?

OFF STAGE VOICE: Four …

BORIS: Optimistic.

OFF STAGE VOICE: Three…

BORIS: But not hubristic.

OFF STAGE VOICE: Two…

TONY: Hi Boris! It's Tony! Break a leg!

OFF STAGE VOICE: One…

BORIS: What?

OFF STAGE VOICE: And, go Huw!

    TONY vanishes.

HUW: My guests tonight are Sir Boris Johnson, hotly tipped to be the next Prime Minister and the Reverend Michael Gove. Sir Boris if I can start with you. Why should we trust you? You wanted out now you want back in. You're a charlatan aren't you?

BORIS: Good evening Huw look this is a critical point in our history. It is, the economy stupid, it always has been, and I will not apologize for my, political suppleness, my willingness to change.

HUW: Are you a 'selfish, opportunistic liar' as one Tory MP said this week?

BORIS: Of course not but look this whole, drama, is not about me it's about this great nation of ours, where we go next and if we return to the bosom of our European friends huge advantages await.

HUW: Such as?

BORIS: Er. Lorry safety. Huge strides to be made. In the field. Of lorry safety. I'm HGV positive!

MICHAEL *turns into* **CHURCHILL.**

WINSTON: Make the case boy.

CHURCHILL *turns back into* **MICHAEL.**

BORIS: Right. The Benefits of Brentry, indeed, the Brenefits of Brentry, that's what they are, Brenefits. The Brenefits, of Brenrty. Will be huge. Huw. Britain is a great country.

HUW: Okay. How easy will it be to re-join though? Coz leaving, wasn't exactly, straightforward was it.

BORIS: True. Someone, once said, leaving the EU, was like, reversing a vasectomy. It was that complicated. And yes, re-joining, would be like, reversing, a reverse vasectomy. There's an image. Yuh.

HUW: Thank you for that.

VOICE OF THATCHER: You, are a Judas!

BORIS: Shut up!

HUW: I beg your pardon?

BORIS: Nothing. Sorry. Hello? Yup.

HUW: And what's the view from the pulpit as it were? Here we are, tearing ourselves apart still.

MICHAEL: What we should remember Huw, is that we all, simply want what's best for our country. When we tear ourselves apart as you say we do it, not out of hatred, but love: love for our country. We simply can't agree that's all. And we should also remember that things aren't nearly as bad as they seem. Let's remember how lucky we are, to be British. We have the best everything. The best countryside, music, sport, museums, teachers, poets, writers, comedians, doctors, scientists, designers, architects I could go on. This, you see, is simply God's way of testing us. And eventually, it will be seen for what it is. A tiny cosmic bump in the road. Compared to all we've been through. The centuries, of war, famine, plague and pestilence. We survived, everything. And we will survive this. We'll be fine. This precious stone, set in a silver sea, will be fine. Because this is how democracy works. And yes when you see it up close, democracy, in action, can be ugly. It's like, two warthogs mating. Painful. Unpredictable. Off putting. But in essence. A beautiful thing.

HUW: Well I'm not sure where that gets us –

MICHAEL: But I will say this Huw –

HUW: Please do.

MICHAEL: I think we too often fail to admit when we've got it wrong – .

HUW: *(Nipping in.)* – Ah! So you're saying we were wrong to leave in the first place?

MICHAEL: No. It was right at the time and faced with the same circumstances I'd do the same again. But what I didn't know then, was how things would pan out. There's been a fundamental shift which we didn't foresee and I think it right and proper the British people be given a chance to respond.

HUW: So you're saying – . What are you saying?

MICHAEL: There perhaps, should be. A referendum. On re-joining.

HUW: This must be music to your ears.

BORIS: Indeed! A symphony! A lush, European, symphony played on flutes, trombones and violins. But it is of course not over, 'til the fat lady – , sorry, the plus-sized lady, sorry the XXL, non-gender specific person, sings.

HUW: So Reverend who should lead us into that referendum? The man sitting opposite? No reservations this time? We all know what happened last time.

Reverend Gove?

Pause.

HUW: Let me ask again. Have you any reservations about the man opposite you?

BORIS: Not this time he hasn't.

HUW: For the third time. Have you, any reservations, about the man opposite you?

BORIS: Oh God.

MICHAEL: I have. Some.

HUW: Okay…

MICHAEL: I have listened, to Him.

HUW: You're watching the BBC Amazon News Channel.

MICHAEL: And I have to say, some of the old doubts. Have returned.

HUW: Okay…

BORIS: He's talking about Brexit. That's what he doubts. He doubts we should have, Brexited? Is that a verb? In the first place.

MICHAEL: Actually. My doubts. Concern. Sir Boris.

BORIS: Jesus Christ.

HUW: Sorry about that. Carry on Reverend.

BORIS: Exactly. Carry on Reverend!

MICHAEL: When one assesses the suitability of someone to be Prime Minister I believe you have to look at character, first and foremost. What motivates them. And I have been talking to, and indeed, reading a book by, a very impressive young woman –

BORIS: *(To himself, almost.)* Caitlin.

HUW: I beg your pardon?

BORIS: Look. That's just, rubbish. And hold on! Yes! I've a letter! From Michael! Saying he supports me!

HUW: Would you like to read it to us?

BORIS: With pleasure.

BORIS – *ticking time bomb* – *turns out pockets. They're empty.*

BORIS: Huurghh. Must have dropped it.

HUW: Can you, enlighten us, Reverend Gove?

MICHAEL: Do you know what you should be asking Huw? With respect? What you should be asking, is, is it worth the risk, of electing the person next to me? I mean I admire Boris don't get me wrong. I don't admire the way he conducts his private life but that's just a personal view. But what would it say about us, as a nation, if we made someone like him our leader, again?

HUW: What would it say?

MICHAEL: It would say. We were reckless. Dangerously reckless.

HUW: Can you elaborate?

MICHAEL: People like him. Because he's funny. Some people. But what he could do to this country. Might not be funny at all.

BORIS: How long'd it take you to come up with that you four eyed CUNT!

MICHAEL: And that is why, tonight, I am announcing my return to front line politics. I have decided, after much –

    BORIS *explodes, punches* **MICHAEL** *mid-sentence.*

HUW: Oh Boy. Let's take a break.

BORIS: I'll give you a break you bloody arse.

HUW: Try it on with me Sonny and I'll wipe the floor with you. *(To* **CAMERA**.*)* Back in a moment.

    BORIS *backs down. Red 'on air' light turns off.* **MICHAEL** *moans.*

HUW: Are you all right Michael?

MICHAEL: *(Exits, staggering, making sign of cross.)* Forgive us our trespasses… as we forgive those…

HUW: You just ended your career.

    HUW *exits.* **BORIS** *blank, shocked: all is lost.*

NEWS VOICE: – breaking news Sir Boris Johnson has pulled out of the contest to lead the Tory party after an alleged assault on the Reverend Michael Gove. *(Fade.)* It's understood Reverend Gove has declined to press charges…

SCENE SEVEN

BORIS, *shoulders slumped, makes a call.*

FEMALE MOBILE VOICE: Jack Carson Agency?

BORIS: Put Jack on. It's Boris.

MOBILE VOICE: Who?

BORIS: Boris. Bojo. Boris Johnson.

Hold music. **BORIS** *fiddles with his hair, talks to himself.*

BORIS: "If you can wait, and not be tired of waiting…yuh! If you can wait and not be tired of waiting." Thank you, Rudyard. Too right Rudyard. Too right Ruddy. Too ruddy right Ruddy!

MOBILE VOICE: Just putting you through.

AGENT: Boris?

BORIS: Jack! Anything come in for me?

AGENT: Are you fucking joking?

BORIS: Is this still about me punching Gover? He was bloody well asking for it.

AGENT: Mate you're toxic.

BORIS: What about the book deal?

AGENT: Off the table.

BORIS: Why?

AGENT: Leaving aside the GBH, haven't you seen, Caitlin's everywhere? They can't wait to read her book. She does not hold back. Something about a wardrobe and a key sticking out.

BORIS: Yeah yeah all right.

AGENT: Bunny's after a book deal too. Maybe you should go into hibernation.

BORIS: I WILL NOT GO GENTLY!

AGENT: Up to you.

BORIS: Is there nothing?

AGENT: There is one thing.

BORIS: I'll do it.

AGENT: It's an ad.

BORIS: Great.

AGENT: A shit one.

BORIS: Great.

AGENT: And the joke will be very much on you.

BORIS: I'll do it I'll do it. Could lead to something.

Jack hangs up. **BORIS** *is now on the set of an advert.*

TV PRODUCER VOICE: All right Boris. Ready for a take?

BORIS: It's only over when they put you in the ground.

TV PRODUCER VOICE: Boris. BORIS! You ready for a take?

BORIS: Hrrgh.

AGENT: Are you all right? You look a bit – .

BORIS: I'm fine. Is this gonna be good? I wannna make it, classy.

TV PRODUCER VOICE: And do the voice, right? Okay. Ready everyone? Action!

BORIS: *(Churchillian voice.)* We shall insure you on the beaches. We shall insure you on the landing grounds. We shall insure you in the fields and in the streets. We shall insure you in the hills.

(Normal voice.) There are many insurers out there. But only one that really packs a punch. Booof! Churchill. Beware, of imitations.

TV VOICE: And...cut!

BORIS: Was that all right?

The set starts to creak. An assistant clears the props etc.

BORIS: I thought that was pretty good.
Do you wanna go for drink later?
Bloody hell. Where is everyone?

Darkness. Smoke. More creaking. A vision of hell, with **TONY**, **MARGARET** *and* **WINSTON** *in it.*

BORIS: Where am I?

MARGARET: The other place.

BORIS: The House of Lords?

MARGARET: It's where we all end up. Treachery! That's what it was! Treachery!

TONY: Can't admit I was wrong. If I admit I was wrong then – . Hi! Hi? Hi.

BORIS: Who else is here?

WINSTON: Angry American guy?

BORIS: What, Donald? Where is he?

MARGARET: Playing Monopoly with Mr. Mugabe.

WINSTON: I could have been President of Europe. I should have been President of Europe.

MARGARET: We're very happy that we shall soon be leaving this place in a very much better state than when we came here all those years ago.

TONY: It may not happen you know. Ever. You may never get what you want.

BORIS: Yes I will. Yes I will. I, will!

BLACK OUT

ENDS

Salamander Street

Also available from Jonathan Maitland

Dead Sheep

Paperback 9781913630782
eBook 9781913630775

It is 1989 and a seemingly invincible Prime Minister has sacked Geoffrey Howe, her Foreign Secretary. She apparently had nothing to fear from him: his speaking skills had, famously, been compared to those of a dead sheep. But, a year later, inspired by his wife Elspeth – whose relationship with Thatcher was notoriously frosty – Howe overcame his limitations to destroy Mrs Thatcher with one of the great political speeches. The staging of *Dead Sheep* is a drama tinged with tragedy and comedy. Its themes – loyalty, love, political morality and Britishness – are as relevant today as they were a quarter of a century ago.

www.ingramcontent.com/pod-product-compliance
Lightning Source LLC
Jackson TN
JSHW031524131224
75386JS00044B/1742